Powerful Communication

Influence, Persuasion, and Communication Skills You Need to Have

Ric Thompson

Ric Thompson

**Just to say Thank You for Purchasing this Book I want
to give you a gift 100% absolutely FREE**

A Copy of My Special Report "*Outsource Time*"

**Go to www.DoneForYouSolutions.com/OutsourceTime
to Receive Your FREE Gift**

Table of Contents

Introduction

I want to thank you and congratulate you for purchasing, "*Powerful Communication: Influence, Persuasion, and Communication Skills You Need to Have.*"

This book contains proven steps and strategies for improving your communication skills and how to use those skills to achieve your goals and live your dreams. Whether you are a business owner, leader, or entrepreneur, communication is critical and if your communication abilities are limited, your potential for success will also be limited.

After reading this book, you will understand why powerful communication is so important, what communication should look like, how it goes wrong, and why active listening is so important. You will have a better understanding of the role body language, intonation, and even tone of voice play in communicating.

If you have big dreams and lofty goals, the key to getting what you want is being able to communicate effectively with the people who can help you achieve your goals and make your dreams come true. Understanding how to craft a message specific to the person who needs to receive it in a way that maneuvers around any filters they have that might blocking it makes it easier to get the right message to the right person at the right time.

And this is, in effect, the point of communicating. When we can communicate effectively, we build rapport which builds trust which helps to enhance and strengthen the relationships we need to get things done. In order to do this in the most effective way possible, you need to be able to identify the other person's communication style and use that information to craft a message and a delivery strategy tailored to that individual or group.

With the help of ***Powerful Communication***, you're on your way to achieving just about anything you can imagine. Thanks again for purchasing, I hope you enjoy it!

Ric Thompson

Communication: How it Works, and How it Doesn't

Not long ago, an international airline created an ad campaign targeting Spanish speakers. It included billboards planted in auspicious places touting that they could fly "en cueros," highlighting the luxurious leather seats available on flights. Unfortunately, as the airline execs later learned the context in which it was used translated to "naked", not leather seating. Even though the message was memorable, it certainly wasn't the message the company wanted to send.

These kinds of communication problems happen all the time. We use words in the wrong context, give instructions that are not clearly understood, say things other than what we mean, or fail to use the resources available to us to ensure the message we are sending is clear. Communication issues can happen for a variety reasons in almost any area of our lives. To demonstrate this, let's look at a few examples.

- A report was filed to an insurance company that began with: "Coming home, I drove into the wrong house and collided with a tree I don't have." What? Did this person really speak as badly as he drove, or was it one of those phone depositions that the interpreter got all wrong? Do you suppose he got paid for the damage after he told the adjuster he didn't mean what was in the report? This is a classic example of how easy it is to struggle to convey a clear message when speaking.

- A well intentioned volunteer for her church often helped type the bulletin. One week a few of her notices got noticed.

o *"For those who have children and don't know it, we have a nursery downstairs."*

o *"Thursday at 5 PM, there will be a meeting of the Little Mother's club. All ladies wishing to be 'little mothers' will meet with the pastor in his study."*

It's amazing how much difference in meaning a misplaced word or some missing punctuation can cause. These are both great examples of how we can misstep when we try to convey a clear message in writing.

In our fast-paced, challenging times, these kinds of errors happen often. Unfortunately, they aren't usually that funny.

The Importance of Communication

This is how communication works – and how it doesn't. If the message being sent isn't clear or if it isn't received as it was intended, the outcome is very likely to be different than the one you had anticipated. And that outcome is all yours to deal with, regardless of where the communication broke down.

Effective communication is at the root of every relationship. When we aren't clear when communicating with our business associates, family or friends, the results can be far-reaching, even devastating. Being able to effectively communicate is so important that it can affect your happiness, career, wealth and overall success. It impacts everything you do, dawn to dusk, every single day. Which means it isn't something you can leave to chance.

Many people, even the most dynamic, in-charge people, take communication for granted though. They expect the people around them to understand them quickly and respond appropriately.

Take a minute to think back to the last time you made one or more of these communication blunders:

- Talking without thinking
- Asking someone do something while they are busy doing something else
- Making a request that didn't result in the outcome you expected
- Giving instructions that had to be repeated

These are all examples of how communication doesn't work. Perhaps, those of us who have been talking, and leading, and doing big things for years are the ones who could most use a reminder about how to do those things well.

If you have big dreams and lofty goals, the key to getting what you want is being able to communicate effectively with the people who can help you achieve your goals and make your dreams come true.

"Fully 85% of your success in life is contained in your ability to communicate effectively with other people." -
Brian Tracy

What it is and Why it Matters to You

From your first cry as a newborn, you begin learning the challenging skills of communication. You learn how to express your desires in a way that gets you what you need. As you grow and learn more advanced communication skills like speaking and writing, your ability to get what you need becomes more and more dependent on those communication skills. Unfortunately, this means you will only be as good at communicating as those who taught you to communicate.

As you mature, your ability to communicate effectively will depend on how well you choose to develop your own skills. Your mastery over your native language, your ability to speak various languages, your choice of words and vocabulary, and so forth, become a product not only of your environment, but of your own choices. And the need for powerful communication has never been more critical to success than it is in our modern world.

One of the most dynamic examples of this need can be seen in an example we've already been having fun with: air travel.

In fact, let's step it up a notch and consider international air travel. Let's pretend you're planning a trip from your hometown to Venice, Italy. Think of the vast network of information required to schedule your trip among planes that travel between thousands of airports. Think of the coordination involved in purchasing and reserving a specific seat on one of those flights. Think of the people who staff the airport, the airline and the plane, many of whom speak different languages.

Dig deeper and consider the communication that has to take place before the plane can even leave the ground. There are air traffic controllers talking to pilots, dispatchers talking to ground crews, gate agents talking to flight attendants, and pilots talking to everyone. There are computers talking to computers and all the humans involved in this process are also communicating with and through computers.

Miraculously, despite all these communication touch points, there is a good chance you will get where you want to go, almost on time – and so will your luggage, most of the time.

This isn't really a miracle, it happens because the "flow" of information that is communicated from the time a passenger books a ticket until she picks up her bags at her destination is a practiced system that is designed to work well.

Do you have a well-defined communication system in place or do you "fly" a little more by the "seat of the pants?" As an entrepreneur, you have a lot in common with the air traffic controllers because the flow of information flowing through your business may be much less predictable...something like this:

> *A DC-10 came in a little hot and thus had an exceedingly long roll out after touching down.*
> *The tower noted: "American 751, make a hard right turn at the end of the runway, if you are able. If you are not able, take the Guadalupe exit off Highway 101, make a right at the lights and return to the airport."*
>
> *Or, on a bad day...*
>
> *"TWA 2341, for noise abatement turn right 45 Degrees."*
> *"Center, we are at 35,000 feet. How much noise can we make up here?"*
> *"Sir, have you ever heard the noise a 747 makes when it hits a 727?"*

Some days, clear communication may just seem over your head.

Powerful communication, one on one, can be surprisingly challenging.

- Have you ever had a great idea that you had the hardest time getting someone else to "see?"

- Have you ever asked someone to do something, had him tell you he would, only to find out later it wasn't done at all like you asked?

- Have you ever given someone driving directions, only to have them call you later – totally lost?

- Have you ever created a plan to meet someone at a particular place and time only to learn they were waiting on you somewhere else?

- Have you ever been the one who got it all wrong?

Of course! We all have had many experiences like this. As a result, we've wasted untold time and money and effort; gotten frustrated and even damaged relationships. Stuff happens and we all make mistakes, but many of these mishaps can be managed and even eliminated when we learn how to communicate clearly.

But how can you tell if you are communicating clearly and effectively? The evaluation tool on the next page will help you gauge how you are doing in a variety of different communication settings. Once you know where you are doing well communicating and where you are falling down, you will be able to apply the lessons in this guide to focus in on improving your communication skills where they will benefit you the most.

The Communication Evaluator Part I

Give yourself 1 point for each item you answer in the affirmative.

Communication Basics

☐ I believe that the more powerful my communications, the better.

☐ I'm a confident communicator.

☐ I know how to listen actively.

☐ I rarely interrupt other people.

☐ I rarely have communication mix-ups or challenges.

Basics score out of 5: _____

Communication Challenges

☐ Other people clearly understand my communication most of the time.

☐ The outcomes and results that happen after I make a request or give an instruction are most often those I expect.

☐ I'm comfortable meeting new people.

☐ I can keep a conversation going with someone I just met.

☐ I can always be proud of my written communication.

☐ I communicate with people easily, regardless of their personality style.

☐ People seem to feel better about me and about themselves after our communications.

☐ I know how to ask questions when I need clarification.

☐ I'm familiar with the filters that get in the way of people hearing my messages.

☐ I'm aware of communication challenges that keep coming up for me and what to do about them.

Challenges score out of 10: _____

Communicating to Groups

☐ I often speak to groups of people.

☐ I look forward to speaking to groups because that format of communication is often important.

☐ When I speak to people, I feel confident and positive.

☐ When I speak to people, I get a chance to get my ideas across.

☐ When I speak to people, I receive good feedback.

Groups score out of 5: _____

Communicating Professionally

☐ I'm comfortable giving feedback to people who work with and for me.

☐ I'm comfortable receiving feedback from peers and employees.

☐ My instructions to others are consistently followed and completed, as I need them to be.

☐ My peers share their ideas and goals and seem eager to hear mine.

☐ I can quickly "figure out" how to approach other people about business.

Professional score out of 5: _____

Communicating as a Leader

- ☐ I believe that clear communication is a crucially important aspect of leadership.
- ☐ I'm confident working with other people at meetings.
- ☐ I lead efficient, clear and productive meetings.
- ☐ I'm confident that when I communicate new ideas and goals to people I lead, they will become excited and contribute to the goals.
- ☐ When I speak as a leader, people respect what I have to say.

Leadership score out of 5:

Scoring

Overall Score	
Basics	
Challenges	
Groups	
Professional	
Leadership	
TOTAL:	

Notice the areas that your communication skills need the most work. The chart below will interpret your current feelings about yourself as a communicator.

Evaluation	
27-30	You believe you have a solid mastery of communication, while there may be room for improvement.
20-26	Good communication skills are indicated with a few areas that need work.
15-19	Your communication ability needs work – you have areas of weakness.
0-14	Powerful communication is a challenge for you, but that is about to change!

After having gone through the evaluation, ask yourself the following questions.

What have you learned about yourself from this process?

Do any areas stand out as strengths or weaknesses? If so, what are they?

Communication Gets Us What We Want

We learn as kids in school that communication sets humans apart from other highly functioning animals. It makes sense that the better we communicate, the more likely we are to get what we want in life, make a difference in our world, and be happy and satisfied at all levels. Communication is, without doubt, the most important skill required to live successfully in our competitive world.

> *"You can have brilliant ideas, but if you can't get them across, your ideas won't get you anywhere." - Lee Iacocca*

Communication takes place when two or more people exchange information. Once a message is created and spoken or written or acted, it must be heard or read or seen by someone else for communication to have taken place. It must always be a two way street to be effective. This is why communication is often ineffective or even absent – the message was sent, but it was never received in the first place!

"The problem with communication ... is the illusion that it has been accomplished." – *George Bernard Shaw*

You've most likely experienced the frustration of feeling like you're "talking to a wall" when you speak. Unless we get some confirmation that our message has been received, we can't know for sure that we've communicated. Perhaps the most crucial thing you can do to be an effective communicator is to remember that your message is not as important as whether – and how – it is received. Quite simply – you haven't communicated until someone has received your message, so we'll spend most of the book on that issue.

"Most conversations are simply monologues delivered in the presence of a witness." - *Margaret Miller*

Think back to personal examples of communications challenges. Make a list of examples of communication challenges you've had. What was your role in the communication effort? Can you remember what caused the disconnect? You can use the table below to document previous challenges to see if you can identify any patterns.

Situation	Your Role	Reason for Problem

As you go through this book, reflect back on these situations and consider how the outcome may have been different if you had known then what you are learning now. This will also help you understand how similar communication situations can go differently in the future.

How Communication Happens

Think about the process of communication. Basically, it's made up of three parts:

- the sender of the message
- the message
- the receiver of the message

Seems pretty straightforward, so how can there be so many ways for it to go wrong? Before we count them, let's consider all the different pieces of the communication puzzle. In addition to the parts of the communication process, there are also other factors involved in any communication.

They are:

- The content of the message – is it good news or bad, interesting or boring, threatening or supportive, clear or muddled, accurate or not, and so forth.

- The intonation, style, attitude, body language, timing, etc. of the sender's voice.

- The attitude, mood and circumstances, etc. of the receiver.

The various multiples of these factors mean that there are many, many things that can get in the way of effective and productive communication. In fact, there are more reasons why a simple request, question or comment could be misinterpreted than there are reasons for it to be received as intended.

So, your job is to anticipate those potential pitfalls – and avoid them.

List various situations you can think of in your current life interactions that require you to communicate accurately, effectively... powerfully. What situations do you find yourself in that require you to function at your best or serious negative results could be the outcome?

Situation	Your Role	Serious Potential

Think about people you admire as communicators. List the things that you like about their communication styles.

Person	Style	What You Like

As you become more aware of communication in general, and just what makes it powerful, you'll begin to understand that it is more complicated than we think.

In the next section we'll examine the reasons why whatever can go wrong often does when it comes to communicating.

What *Should* Happen But Often *Doesn't*

"Precision of communication is important, more important than ever, in our era of hair trigger balances, when a false or misunderstood word may create as much disaster as a sudden thoughtless act." - *James Thurber*

Let's take a deeper look at those three components of communication and your control over each of them.

The Sender

First, let's consider what goes into the Sender's verbal communication. It's interesting to think about what happens when you say something to someone. A study completed by Albert Mehravian, a UCLA professor, found that the meaning of an interaction can be broken down into the following:

- Facial and body language
- Vocal intonation and inflection
- The words used

What matters most to you is the percentage that each component plays in the total communication:

- Body language was most important at 55%.
- Next was vocal intonation and inflection at 38%.
- Finally, the words contributed only 7% to the total exchange.

This is EXTREMELY important to you as a communicator! It means that no matter how hard you try to find just the right words, your messages will be conveyed by the details that other people see in your behavior and hear in your voice more than the words that you use.

When you think about the results of the UCLA study, what do you think you could do to improve as the sender of messages? Make a list, separating your thoughts into the three categories.

Facial and Body Language	Vocal Intonations and Inflection	Words You Use

Now, considering that the first two columns carry a value of 93%, have you come up with significant ideas for how you might improve those two aspects of what happens when you send a message?

Take another look at your list. Can you add any more ideas?

The Message

> *"Wise men talk because they have something to say; fools, because they have to say something."* – Plato

What can go wrong with a message? This topic could be a book of its own! Study these questions – and review them every time you have an important or written message to send. Soon, they will become a part of your normal communication process.

- Are you saying what you mean or, are you "dancing" around a topic and not sending a clear message? This point is particularly important when you're giving instructions or asking someone to do something.

- What is the best way to say EXACTLY what you mean? (Later in this section, we'll consider validating what the Receiver thinks he or she heard.)

- Are you speaking clearly and loud enough to be heard? Or, are you mumbling and not even looking at the receiver, oblivious as to whether you were heard or not?

- Are you speaking in a "language" and words that the receiver can understand? Or, are you using lingo, idioms, professional language or big words that are meaningless to the receiver?

- Will your content pass the "filters" of the receiver? (more on this coming up) Or, will the message never be received at all?

- Does your intonation and body language match the message? Or, are you providing a confusing, contradictory image that doesn't make sense?

- Is your timing appropriate for the content and importance of the message? Or, have you picked a time when the receiver is busy doing something and unable to listen? Are you trying to make a point that should be done in private or at a time when you have the receiver's total attention?"

- Does your message matter? Or, are you just talking about "nothing?"

You read earlier about the "flying naked" billboard. Below are some other examples of corporate bloopers. Now if something like this happened at your company, what would you do to make sure bloopers like these never made it off your drawing board?

- Pepsi's "Come alive with the Pepsi Generation" in China translated into "Pepsi brings your ancestors back from the grave."

- The Coca-Cola name in China was first read as "Ke-kou-ke-la", meaning "Bite the wax tadpole" or "female horse stuffed with wax", depending on the dialect. Coke then researched 40,000 characters to find a phonetic equivalent "ko-kou-ko-le" translating into "happiness in the mouth."

- Coors used its slogan, "Turn It Loose," in Spanish, where the translation was read as "Suffer From Diarrhea."

- Scandinavian vacuum manufacturer Electrolux used the following in an American campaign:"Nothing sucks like an Electrolux."

- And, you may have heard Frank Perdue's chicken slogan, "It takes a strong man to make a tender chicken," that translated into Spanish meant, "It takes an aroused man to make a chicken affectionate."

Even if you aren't running an international ad campaign, you have messages that matter, both spoken and written. You can make sure you – and people who answer to you – get it right. Think about what kind of quality controls you can put in place to make sure the messages you send are the ones you intend. Do the same regarding the messages that go out from people who work for you or represent you.

TIP: If you send marketing emails, pay particular attention to this exercise. It's amazing how many companies come up with clever marketing ideas that they send out to huge lists of people with spelling, grammar and content errors that cause the potential customer to simply cringe and... delete!

The Receiver

"To effectively communicate, we must realize that we are all different in the way we perceive the world and use this understanding as a guide to our communication with others." – Tony Robbins

Remember the air traffic controller analogies from earlier? What if you were an experienced pilot and heard the tower report something like this:

> *"American 261, you have traffic at 10 o'clock, 6 miles!" Then your rookie co-pilot answered back:*
> *"This is American 261. Give us another hint! We have digital watches!"*

Time out! Hopefully, the rookie was kidding, but it is true that ENDLESS crazy things can go wrong with the receiver of a message.

In your goal to improve communication, you can control yourself and your message, but you cannot always control how the receiver gets and interprets the message. Since we established previously that communication is a two way street and that it hasn't happened until it's gone full circle, you need to pay particular attention to the receivers of your messages. We're going to spend extra time on the receiving end of messages, because that is usually the most complicated and where things can go very, very wrong.

When the receiver hears a message, it is instantly (and unconsciously, for the most part) filtered in a variety of ways. Let's consider some of these filters so that you, as a message sender, can have a better understanding of what you can do to penetrate them.

Language
Obviously, when the message is spoken in a language we understand, we're most likely to "get" it. "Speaking the same language" also means using words and accents that can be understood. Messages sent in the same language by a person with a different accent or style are often left to interpretation by the receiver. But even when communicating in different languages, it can often be done using almost 100% body language and intonation. Miscues can be challenging when people from different cultures, customs or dialects are misunderstood. If a receiver who has a different background from yours seems troubled or confused, it might be good to ask whether they understood your message.

Pre-Occupation
Many times, messages are sent to a receiver who's not expecting them at the moment. (This is almost always the case with telephone calls emails or text messages.) When the receiver is busy doing something – or even thinking about something – he or she will be interrupted by your message. The receiver must stop whatever they are currently occupied

with and occupy themselves with your message. But this doesn't always happen – or it may not happen quickly enough for them to hear and process your message. "Breaking pre-occupation" is often the first hurdle in communicating. Make sure you are getting through!

State

The physical and emotional condition of the receiver at the time the message is received can create a very strong filter. If the receiver is not well or happy, the message may only be partially heard or it may not be received at all. If they are alert, happy, and/or already paying attention to you, the message is much more likely be quickly received. It is normal for a disinterested or uncaring receiver to generalize or summarize the message in their mind, which may lead to misinterpretation.

Values and Beliefs

Another filter for messages can be found in the receiver's values and beliefs. This filter applies more to some messages than others. If the message is philosophical or political or involves ethics or morals, this filter will be triggered. If the message is in harmony with the receiver's values, it is more likely be received clearly and acted upon. If it is counter to their values and beliefs, it may be misunderstood, ignored, or even received and acted upon in different ways than the sender intended.

Values have a great impact on how we evaluate and act on information. Values and beliefs are particularly important when the communication is between people who don't know each other and the messages may be sensitive

Memory

Memory plays a very important role in human communication. Short-term memory enables the conversation to be completed – and acted upon later if need be. Longer-term memory contributes to communication in the form of experiences, points of reference and the intelligence to assign context to the message. Moreover, experiences help us react and give feedback, whether negative or positive, to certain topics during a conversation. You will obviously send different messages to people who are old enough and experienced enough to have memories of data and situations that they can understand and take action on the messages.

Experience

The receiver's experiences with you specifically, and with people who may be categorized like you (family, profession, sex, age, interests, etc.) create filters for messages. These experiences may be positive or negative and therefore influence how the message is interpreted and acted upon. Not all of the receiver's experiences will be correctly applied to you or your message, which can create a false filter. False filters can make it difficult for your message to be received the way you intend it to be. This filter is linked to memory and may be difficult for you to work around since you won't even be aware that it exists. If you're having communication challenges with a particular person, consider whether there might be something causing them to "filter you out" as a result of a previous experience. In this case, you might even ask: "Is there a problem?"

Miscommunications easily occur when one or more of these filters get in the way of the messages being received. Good communicators know to watch for these kinds of misinterpretations by the receiver and to continuously course correct.

So, what can you do to overcome these kinds of challenges, both as the Sender and when you are the Receiver?

Think about communication challenges that seem to keep coming up for you when communicating with various people. Make a list of those things that seem to happen over and over with the same person. Now make a list of those things that seem to happen over and over with different people. Getting in touch with these recurring challenges, helps get figure out how to avoid them in the future.

Delivery of the Message

Another tool you can use to penetrate the Receiver's filters is to use their learning style to create the most effective message. We all have preferred ways of receiving information and that preference has to do with our learning style. The concept of sensory specific learning preferences, or learning styles, began in the 1920's when psychologists were concerned with teaching dyslexic children and other challenged learners. It has become a widely accepted dimension to understanding human communication.

The three primary learning styles, visual, auditory, and kinesthetic, are modes of receiving and processing information and interacting with others. Generally, each of us prefers to receive information and to interact using one of these three modalities. Our ability to communicate in our preferred style significantly improves the results. The styles are:

Learning Style	Preferences
Visual	Seeing and reading
Auditory	Listening and speaking
Kinesthetic	Touching and doing

It is possible to have a mixed or even a balanced blend of two or three of these styles and we may function better in any of the styles as circumstances change. There is no right vs. wrong or better vs. undesirable style or mix of styles. What matters is that we understand the styles of the people we communicate with frequently so that we can get through their filters and communicate clearly.

Here are questions you can consider to determine someone's style. Place a check by each question to indicate your own preferred style, then tally your score at the bottom to evaluate your preferred learning style.

If you were going to:	Would you prefer this? (Visual)	√	Or, this? (Auditory)	√	Or, this? (Kinesthetic)	√
operate new equipment	read the instructions		listen to an explanation		give it a try	
get travel directions	look at a map		ask for spoken directions		follow your nose and maybe use a compass	
cook a new dish	follow a recipe		call a friend for suggestions		follow your instinct, tasting as you cook	
teach someone something	write instructions		explain verbally		demonstrate and let them try it	
express understanding you'd say this...	I see what you mean		I hear what you are saying		I know how you feel	
ask for instruction you' say this...	show me		tell me		let me try	
direct someone to pay attention to you you'd say this...	watch how I do it		listen to what I'm saying		you try it	
deal with a new product that didn't work	write a letter to the store		phone them		send or take it back to the store	
go somewhere to relax	museums and galleries		music and conversation		playing sport or DIY	
buy a gift	books		music		tools and gadgets	
shop	look at things and imagine owning them		discuss items with clerks		try on clothes and test products	
plan a vacation	read the brochures		listen to recommendations		imagine the experience	
choose a new car	read the reviews		discuss with friends		test-drive what you like	
TOTAL CHECKED						

Do you have one clear preference when it comes to learning style or, are you a mix?

Can you picture a few other people that you communicate with often?

What do you think their styles are?

Would they rather read a memo from you, or hear you talk about it, or give it a try on their own?

How will you use this information to achieve better interactions?

Here are two examples of how business people solved serious communications challenges by using their understanding of preferred learning styles.

1. An entrepreneur who is very visual preferred to communicate through email for its quick and efficient approach. He often found that people he emailed didn't get back to him – even after repeated emails. When asked why he didn't call to get his answers, he responded that it hadn't occurred to him. He was using his preferred style, but once he was able to try another mode, he found that he could often get his problems solved more quickly by tapping into the Receiver's preferred mode.

2. One entrepreneurial partner is auditory, while the other is kinesthetic. Living in two different states, communicating is difficult. The kinesthetic partner found that when she mapped out a new project and emailed it to her partner, they could get on the phone and discuss the details. When he heard a description of the email, he could process

and act on her "to do" approach. His follow up feedback could then be put in an email for her to print and physically "work" on.

Here are typical words that people in each style like to use and that you can use to communicate with them.

Visual	Auditory	Kinesthetic
See	Hear	Feel
Look	Listen	Touch
View	Sounds	Grasp
Appear	Make music	Get hold of
Show	Harmonize	Slip through
Dawn	Tune in/out	Catch on
Reveal	Be all ears	Tap into
Envision	Rings a bell	Make contact
Illuminate	Silence	Throw out
Imagine	Be heard	Turn around
Clear	Resonate	Hard
Foggy	Deaf	Unfeeling
Focused	Melodious	Concrete
Hazy	Dissonance	Get a handle
Picture	Unhearing	Solid

Similarly, here are phrases that are used and useful for each style. Do any sound like the way you or people you know speak?

Visual	Auditory	Kinesthetic
An eyeful	Afterthought	All washed up
Appears to me	Blabbermouth	Boils down to
Beyond a shadow of a doubt	Call on	Chip off the old block
Birds eye view	Clear as a bell	Come to grips with
Catch a glimpse of	Clearly expressed	Control yourself
Clear cut	Describe in detail	Cool/calm/collected
Dim view	Earful	Firm foundations
Flashed on	Enquire into	Get a handle on
Get a perspective on	Give me your ear	Get a load of this
Get a scope on	Give you a call	Get in touch with
Hazy idea	Given amount of	Get the drift of
In light of	Grant an audience	Get your back up
In person	Heard voices	Hand in hand
In view of	Hidden message	Hand in there
Looks like	Hold your tongue	Heated argument
Make a scene	Ideal talk	Hold it
Mental image	Key note speaker	Hold on
Mental picture	Loud and clear	Hot head
Mind's eye	Manner of speaking	Keep your shirt on
Naked eye	Pay attention to	Lay cards on the table
Paint a picture	Power of speech	Pain in the neck
See to it	State your purpose	Pull some strings
Short sighted	To tell the truth	Sharp as a tack
Showing off	Tongue-tied	Slipped my mind
Sight for sore eyes	Tuned in/tuned out	Smooth operator
Staring off into space	Unheard of	So-so
Take a peak	Utterly	Start from scratch
Tunnel vision	Voiced an opinion	Stiff upper lip
Under your nose	Well informed	Stuffed shirt
Up front	Within hearing	Too much hassle
Well defined	Word for word	Topsy-turvy

Learning and communication are closely linked – especially to you, a leader who often must use your communication skills

to train, guide and encourage people to achieve their goals –
and yours.

Be conscious of always considering the Sender, the Message,
and the Receiver. Watch for miscommunications as they are
happening and so you can course-correct your message. For
example, you can clarify by:

- Asking questions
- Watching for body language
- Adjusting your own body language and message
- Obtaining feedback about your message

The next section will consider the most important – and most
often ignored – aspect of great communication: listening.

Listen Up! The Dynamics of Active Listening

"You never really learn much from hearing yourself talk."
– George Clooney

We've discussed the two "players" in the communication game – the sender and the receiver. Typically, these people take turns sending messages. Your role as the receiver is at least as important as your role as the sender, especially if you are the one trying to make a point, control a situation, or convey information. People who don't listen effectively, can't communicate effectively.

"We have two ears and one mouth so that we can listen twice as much as we speak." *– Epictetus*

Listening may be twice as important as talking in good communication. Your initial goal of creating rapport and then trust depends on the power of your listening skills.

The best way to know whether messages have been received and received accurately is to listen carefully to responses from the receivers. In an interaction where the other person's feelings, opinion or information matter, you simply won't know what to SAY back until you HEAR what's on their mind.

Listening first is the key to establishing rapport and to determining what matters to the person you want to communicate with. Listening for information – and then remembering what you hear – requires you to be actively engaged... tuned in! Rapport comes naturally when you show another person that you CARE about their message, feedback and needs by listening carefully.

If communication is key to success… then active listening is key to good communication. Listening is an activity that you must perform consciously – just as you do when you speak. This concept is not a complicated one. Maybe that's what makes it so easy to escape our attention: but, active listening may be the single most important point for you to remember in order to communicate clearly all the time. One subtle but key reason to listen actively is that it causes the other person to be more likely to listen to *you.*

"I know that you believe you understand what you think I said, but I'm not sure you realize that what you heard is not what I meant."
— *Robert McCloskey*

Here are a few tips for active listening:

- Make the conscious choice to listen. "Look like a listener." Your focus is literally where your eyes are.

- Listen for both content and emotion. Concentrate on the message. Don't let your mind wander.

- Ask good questions to understand other people's messages if they are unclear. After you ask a question, LISTEN CAREFULLY! Don't be thinking of another question while you're receiving an answer to the first one. If the message is a complicated, emotional or important one, it may be a good idea to feed back to the sender by saying: "So, I understand that you're saying…."

- Show you're paying attention by making eye contact and nodding or responding as appropriate. Remember how important body language is in communication? When you listen, you "say" a great deal to the other person without even speaking!

We've talked about the importance of clear communication when you are giving instructions or asking someone to do something for you and it is worth noting that your listening skills are as important as the words you choose when you're giving instructions.

Your words may be very clear and appropriate, but the receiver may not get the message for any one of countless reasons. The way to increase your chances of getting the results you want is to ask the other person to confirm or repeat back your instructions. Then, LISTEN carefully to their answer to make sure they're on the right track.

For example, think of instructions you often give to employees, business associates, vendors, or other business people. Then think of questions you might ask them to confirm their understanding of your request. Finally, what answers could they give that would confirm that the message sent was the one received?

Instruction or Request	Feedback Questions	Good Answers
Please help me by getting 10 copies of this report made by Friday	When do you think you'll be able to get to this?	Oh, 10 copies shouldn't be a problem. I should have them Thursday afternoon.

The Art of Conversation

"Seek first to understand, then to be understood." -
Stephen Covey

"The gift of gab," or the ability to enter a new or unfamiliar situation and engage others in conversation, is a widely admired skill. Many people consider it an innate ability but it can easily be learned. This skill can play a vital role in boosting your self-confidence and can be critical in your personal and professional life.

Meeting people for the first time can seem to be a very daunting task if we become preoccupied with ourselves, thinking things like "what should I talk about" and "what shall I say". However, if you think about how *other people* like to communicate and what *they* like to talk about, meeting people for the first time can be an enjoyable experience.

The best conversationalists are also the best listeners. Resist the urge to dominate a conversation. In fact, the person who says the least is often the best communicator. Conversation depends very much on your ability to ask questions and to listen attentively to the answers. Most people are poor listeners because they are busy preparing a reply while the other person is still speaking. During conversation, look like a listener by leaning slightly forward and facing the other person directly. Wait for your turn to speak and don't interrupt.

Conversation and small talk are very easy when you keep in mind the things most people like to talk about:

1. Themselves. The best way to build rapport with someone and to hold a conversation is by encouraging them to talk about their favorite subject - THEMSELVES!

2. Their opinions. People enjoy sharing their opinions about many things. The only word of caution is to avoid any temptation to strongly disagree or become argumentative. This type of interchange doesn't suit casual conversation. If you have a difference of opinion, try asking clarifying questions and LISTEN to the answers – who knows, maybe you'll gain a new a perspective!

3. Their things. You can pay compliments to a person's possessions or interests and be confident that they'll enjoy talking to you.

One thing to remember is that the last thing people want to talk about is YOU – which means that your favorite topic is not on the list! Don't talk about yourself unless the other person asks. Then, keep it short. The less you say, the more people will find you fascinating!

Here's how that works.

> *A friend was traveling from Los Angeles to Sydney with his family for a business trip and vacation. When they got to the hotel about midnight after the long, grueling flight, he was exhausted but couldn't fall asleep. He decided to go to the Club Lounge for a nightcap. One other person was there- a businessman from Germany. Our friend struck up a conversation by asking the man what he did. He said he was a financial consultant who worked with entire countries as clients. Our friend found that intriguing and kept asking the other man questions.*

> *About 45 minutes later the cognac finally worked its magic and our friend was ready for bed. He said farewell and headed for the elevator. As he was leaving, the German man called out to our weary friend and said the strangest thing, "Hey, it was very nice to meet you, you are one of the most fascinating people I've ever met!"*

> *Our friend was dumbfounded because he hadn't said a single word to the man other than to ask him questions – the guy didn't even know his name until he was halfway out the door – but because our friend was genuinely interested in him, asked questions, and LISTENED intently, the man found him fascinating.*

"Those who treasure the sound of their own voice above all others are truly deaf." *– Steve Bersani*

To keep your listening skills sharp, try this active listening exercise once a week. During a conversation, business presentation, or even while watching the news, take detailed written notes. Listen for details that are important to the other person. Watch their body language and listen for the points they THEY consider important. Practice keeping your focus on what they are saying rather than on how you want to respond.

"I can't imagine being effective in business without having some insight into people. Insight demands opening up your senses, talking less and listening more." - *Mark McCormack, What They Don't Teach You at Harvard Business School*

What You're Saying When You're Not *Saying* Anything At All

Any time you're in the presence of another person, you are communicating something to them. It's impossible NOT to send messages – even before you begin speaking.

Body language is your first – and main – communication tool. Remember that 93% of live communication comes from body language and intonation. Only 7% of your message is delivered by the words you choose. This is EXTREMELY important to you as a communicator! No matter how hard you try to find just the right words, your messages will be conveyed more by what people see in your behavior and hear in your voice.

We must always remember that we are constantly communicating through our appearance, mannerisms, tone of voice, gestures, expressions, and so forth. Simply put, it's important that you're aware of your body language to make sure that 93% of what you are saying is aligned with the messages you are trying to send.

Build Good Rapport

> *"The greatest compliment that was ever paid me was when someone asked me what I thought, and attended to my answer." - Henry David Thoreau*

Communication is basically results-oriented. The first step toward your desired result is to build rapport. Once you've built rapport, you are more memorable to others, which can be critical to achieving professional and personal success.

Remember that old adage:

It's not WHAT you know, it's WHO you know!

That means building rapport which is very similar to building a bridge. Rapport bridges the gap between you and the other person and the stronger the bridge, the more it can carry. In a relationship, you can expect more give and take if you have better rapport with the other person.

One quick and easy way to build rapport is to create the "feeling" of having some things in common with your listeners. You can accomplish this very subtly using body language by "patterning" or "mirroring" the other person's actions.

For example:

- Speak slowly if they do—or quickly if that's their style.

- Notice their tone and use a similar one—loud or soft, for example.

- If the other person is standing with their arms folded across their chest, you may cross yours in the same way, or at the wrist.

- Stand if they're standing, sit if they sit.

- Be aware of their breathing pace and attempt to breathe at the same rate.

- If they are interested in details, be detail oriented. If they are more interested in the big picture, concentrate on that. (You'll learn more about this process in the next section.)

• If they provide information about a common experience or interest, tell them that you have those things in common.

This is a SUBTLE skill that you will develop naturally as it feels right for you. Your ability to "mirror" people can become a way of establishing rapport when you put these ideas into place. As you use this tool to establish rapport, remember that it's simply a matter of caring enough about the person you're communicating with to fall into a similar rhythm with them as you talk. Be careful not to "overdo it." You don't want to end up copying the other person and making them feel like they're being mimicked or imitated.

It's been said that people will forget what you say. They'll forget what you do. But, they'll never forget how you make them FEEL. Therefore, making people feel good is the ultimate path to powerful communication.

You can "practice" the concept of mirroring and understand it better by focusing on people you're not actually interacting with. Then, in real life situations, it will be easier for you to watch and listen for the other person's body language and physical messages and subtly mirror them.

To help you understand and practice tuning in to others and mirroring, try this. Choose a presentation, lecture, speech, or even television show in which one person is talking. Watch carefully and make notes of everything you see about the person's patterns. How do they speak? How loud? How fast? What is their body position? What behaviors could you "mirror" if you were speaking with them personally?

Remember, you wouldn't copy this other person, simply "tune in" to be somewhat like them.

Building rapport is about creating a comfort level enabling communication to flow. It's a combination of good manners, paying attention, and sensitivity. It's being nice and helpful and informative. And it sets the stage for people to do business with you, to follow your instructions, to be a resource for you, and so forth.

Public Speaking - The Fate Worse Than Death

Truth is, there are not gravestones that we can find that say anything like:

Poor Michael, the Audience Killed Him as He Spoke

And yet, surveys declare that speaking to a group of people is considered a fate worse than death. As an entrepreneur or leader of any kind, speaking to people casually and formally goes with the territory. As an influencer, you must be able to express your ideas clearly, to enlist the help and loyalty of others, and to direct activities and efforts in line with your goals and objectives.

Whether in business meetings, with customers, in a community meeting, working on a group project, or at a party, you are speaking in public, even if you are not standing behind a podium at the front of the room. Once you have confidence in your ideas and are comfortable communicating, the ability to express those ideas to other people in any setting becomes second nature.

Many of the tips and pointers you'll learn in this section are obvious – but even the most seasoned public speaker can improve their ability. For those who find public speaking uncomfortable, once you've got a few successes under your belt – and you've lived to tell about it – you'll begin to welcome opportunities to express your ideas in public.

First Impressions Come... First

What they say about first impressions is true....

YOU DON'T GET A SECOND CHANCE TO MAKE A GREAT FIRST IMPRESSION.

First impressions are extremely powerful – and they happen in the first THREE SECONDS of seeing someone. This means your "audience", on both casual and professional levels, is never far away. Keep in mind that a first impressions includes everything from how you dress to your body language and it happens before you even get the chance to speak.

Here's what we decide about another person in the first instant:

- Are we impressed by the other person?
- Are we similar to the other person?
- Do we like the other person?

People SEE you before they hear you and they make instant judgments based on your appearance. Like...

- Are you pleasant looking?
- Dressed professionally?
- Clean? Neat?
- Appropriate?
- Groomed?

People will also think of you the way you think of yourself. They will watch your actions to see if they match who you say you are. When the words and actions align, you come across as genuine. When they don't, it can be off-putting and make you seem insincere.

Believability is one of the most important impressions that you must make on any audience. Even a young child will discount you if they don't believe you. Audiences of any age will "tune out" if you're not believable. To be believable, the things you say must match the way you look and sound. If you say you're a professional with an important message, you'd better look and sound like a knowledgeable pro. If you tell a group of kids you're their new soccer coach, you'd better be dressed for the part and also wear a big smile. Similarly, if you look nervous, frightened, embarrassed or unpleasant, people simply won't want to listen to you. Be who you say you are, and the message will be much closer to hitting its mark.

When you introduce yourself to others, be conscious of communicating whatever it is that you want them to know about you. When you're introducing yourself to a group, be clear about why your message is something they'll want to hear.

Body language is even more important when you're in front of a group. When you address groups of people, remember to:

- Control the tone of your voice. If it's not pleasant, people will literally tune you out. If you speak too softly or quickly, they won't understand you – and won't try for long. People naturally listen to a charismatic voice. You can cultivate a strong voice by paying attention to how you sound – and how other people sound. Project your voice when you want to be heard. Stand up straight and literally throw your voice to the back of the room – without shouting. Breathe deeply and regularly – this will also help keep you relaxed. If public speaking is an important part of your life, you might consider voice training or coaching.

- Allow your enthusiasm, energy and sincerity to be projected in your message. Pause and repeat yourself to emphasize important points. If your goal is to obtain an emotional connection with your audience, that emotion must begin with you.

- Speak a little more slowly than you would in conversation but keep the pace natural.

- Be prepared. Whether you actually prepare a speech or are involved in an impromptu meeting, speak only about topics you understand. If you don't know what you're talking about… don't talk. It's better to attend a meeting as an interested listener than as someone who steals other people's time and patience with irrelevant or ignorant chatter.

- Be conscious of your appearance and how people see you. Make sure that your body posture is appropriate for the situation, and that you are standing or sitting in such a manner that you can be clearly heard. (It's usually best to stand – regardless of the setting.) Be completely conscious of your body language and eliminate any nervous gestures.

- Make sure your message is:

  1.   clear

2.   communicated in terms your audience can understand – no doublespeak
3.   true, current and not exaggerated or detrimental
4.   sincere
5.   consistent with your goals, beliefs and previous messages

"Be sincere; be brief; be seated." – *Franklin Delano Roosevelt*

Talk to three people who have heard you speak in front of people. Ask for their candid feedback about:

- How well you established rapport
- The impression that you made
- Your tone of voice
- Your enthusiasm and energy
- Your pace
- Your preparation
- Your appearance
- Do you have any habits (good or not) that are noticeable in your presentation?

Consider their responses and notice the points (positive or not) that they all agreed on. Think about how you can use this feedback to improve your public speaking skills.

Leaders are Communicators
Great Leaders are Great Communicators

Once you feel good about speaking in public, you can further develop this important leadership skill. Here are some tips that will help you to be as outstanding when speaking in front of people as you can be.

1.   Your posture. A podium is often provided in a
      formal public speaking situation, particularly if the
      speaker is using a microphone or notes. If you
      speak from a podium, remember to stand tall
      behind it. Avoid the temptation to lean forward
      on the podium. Whether you use a podium or
      not, it's always a good idea to move forward
      toward the audience so that you appear to be one
      of them, rather than removed. If you are speaking
      without a podium, you can stress a point or
      become more intimate with listeners by moving
      toward or even among them. Your upright,
      positive, but relaxed posture will tell a great deal
      about your confidence, sincerity and likeability.
      Try not to use notes or a prepared script. This
      approach will be much easier and you will appear
      much stronger.

2.   Interact with the audience. Depending on your
      situation, you can create greater rapport and value
      for your listeners by either taking their questions
      or asking them questions to inform yourself about
      them and involve them in the topic. One caution
      is that an audience member may want to "steal"
      your time or take over your presentation. You
      must remain the leader in this situation.
      Complementing the listeners, identifying with
      them and helping them are sincere ways to
      improve rapport and your own success.

3.   Make eye contact. Regardless of your audience
      size, each person should feel spoken "to," not
      "at." You achieve this by looking each one in the
      eye, as much as possible.

4.   Use humor. Most people would rather not hear a
      joke than hear a bad one just for the sake of

"inserting humor." If you are a person with a good sense of humor, and the topic fits, let your humor shine through. If humor is not your strong point, don't try to be someone you're not. Humor for humor's sake is usually not advisable; humor that flows naturally is almost always advisable. Certainly, it is wise to take your topic seriously, and yourself lightly. If there is a story or anecdote that makes a point for you, whether humorous or not, stories are often a great way to convey an idea.

5.   Word choices. Remember your audience. Always avoid words that might offend ANYONE in your audience. Avoid words or jargon that they may not understand. Avoid using 30 words when 3 will do. Avoid biases and prejudices that are inappropriate.

6.   Timing. Much can be said by saying nothing. A well-timed pause can be a very valuable tool in making a point. Use timing to deliver humor, to let a point sink in, to wait for questions. Prepare your thoughts so that your point is made at the right time – not too early or too late. Use timing in your physical movements to capture attention and rapport. As a rule, any presentation is improved by being short and to the point.

7.   Practice or rehearse. An important, planned presentation is worth preparing to deliver. Although a spontaneous speech is better to listen to than one that is read or delivered from memory, you can write the points, flow, humorous thoughts and ideas and then practice your delivery for the best possible result.

Return to the exercise earlier in this section in which you asked for three evaluations of your presentation skills. Now that you've considered these tips for GREAT presentation skills, what can you add to the feedback you received before? What feedback will you look for in the future to help you be confident you're delivering great presentations?

On the other hand... look at the bright side. Even the smartest and most practiced speakers often misspeak, choose the wrong words, and create mixed messages. And, they LIVED to talk again! We'll end this section assuring you that even a bad presentation before a group isn't really a fate worse than death.

Here are a few presidential bloopers that illustrate that even the most powerful person on the planet with a room full of speechwriters can stumble and say the wrong thing – and live to blunder another day.

"It's no exaggeration to say the undecideds could go one way or another." - George H.W. Bush

"People who like this sort of thing will find this the sort of thing they like." - Abraham Lincoln

"I know how hard it is for you to put food on your family." – George W. Bush

"There is a mandate to impose a voluntary return to traditional values." – Ronald Reagan

"This is still the greatest country in the world if we just will steel our wills and lose our minds." – Bill Clinton

"If Lincoln were alive today, he'd roll over in his grave." – Gerald Ford

"When a great many people are unable to find work, unemployment results." - Calvin Coolidge

"Solutions are not the answer." — Richard Nixon

Personal Communication Styles

"Enough about you... let's hear about me." - Heimel

People are different and unique and it follows that when the Sender of a message uses the style that best suits the Receiver, communication will be more successful. We can't predict precisely how to best communicate with a specific person in any given circumstance – that's why listening and "course correcting" based on feedback are so important. However, there are predictable styles that you can easily identify that "fit" most people. Once you understand the differences, you can easily "target" your own style to match someone else's preferred style. You can also get clear about what your own style is. How do you function best as a message receiver? You will soon understand how your style impacts your interactions with others.

Everyone is different and wants to be dealt with on their own terms. Some people want you to get to the bottom line and get there ASAP. Some people want to know exactly how you got to the bottom line before they agree with you or even receive any more of your messages. Some people prefer to discuss the weather and leave the bottom line alone. And, some people would prefer to discuss it all over a friendly cup of coffee while you exchange ideas.

Your job is to figure out which style your friend or new business acquaintance – or even relative – prefers, and then deal with them accordingly. You need to be flexible, but the process is simple once you understand it.

Personality types have been studied at length over the years with improved communication in mind. There is a general consensus that four predominant styles can be observed.

Although these styles are labeled with various descriptive adjectives and titles, the basic styles have remained constant.

We'll use the following labels:
- Expressive
- Amiable
- Driver
- Analytical

The easiest way to identify each style is to lay out a system to help you determine each one.

To get to the COMMUNICATION STYLES, we'll first consider four different PERSONALITY style descriptors. Once you have the personality styles figured out, you'll translate them into communication styles.

The Personality styles are:
- Dominant or Easy Going and
- Informal or Formal

A DOMINANT person might be:
- Confident
- In-charge
- Extroverted
- Talkative
- Fast-paced
- Make definitive statements
- Assertive
- Outgoing
- Verbal
- Someone who tells things

And, an EASY GOING person might be:
- Subtle
- Compliant

- Introverted
- Quiet
- Deliberate
- Ask questions
- Accepting
- Passive
- Thoughtful
- Good listener

An individual will be EITHER Dominant or Easy Going MOST OF THE TIME. You can see that the characteristics are fairly opposite.

So, think of someone you'd like to "figure out" and ask yourself where they would fit on the continuum below.

Are they more Dominant or Easy Going?

If they are VERY Dominant, mark an "X" far to the left near the 10, or more to center left – or even in the middle of the line if they are not so Dominant or even toward the 0 if they switch frequently. Or, if they are very Easy Going, mark the line as it fits their personality to the right. These descriptors don't imply that a person displays all of the listed descriptors, but if they seem to fit in general, you can be confident that you're describing their personality.

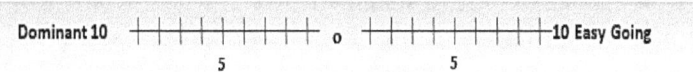

An Informal person's style could be described as:
- Spontaneous
- Emotional
- Intuitive

- Responsive
- Impulsive
- Demonstrative
- Interactive
- Verbal
- Unstructured

A Formal person's style would be:
- Withholding their feelings
- Reserved
- Self-controlled
- Cautious/disciplined
- Intellectual
- Conservative
- Organized
- Structured
- Distant

Again, one personality is USUALLY either more Informal or Formal – not both. These characteristics are totally different. So, consider the person again, and mark this continuum with an "X" according to where they usually fit. This time, we'll use a vertical line…

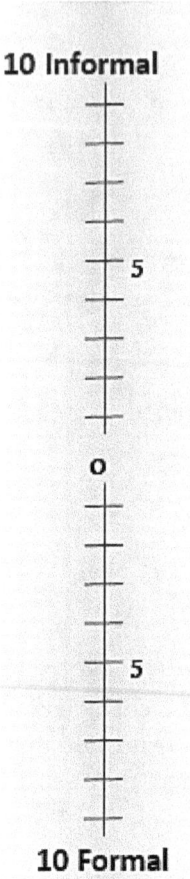

10 Informal

5

o

5

10 Formal

In order to determine a communication style (Expressive, Amiable, Driver or Analytical), we overlay these two continuums to create a North vs. South and West vs. East chart. The personality characteristics you just identified by your two "X's" can now meet to form another point on our new chart, as shown below.

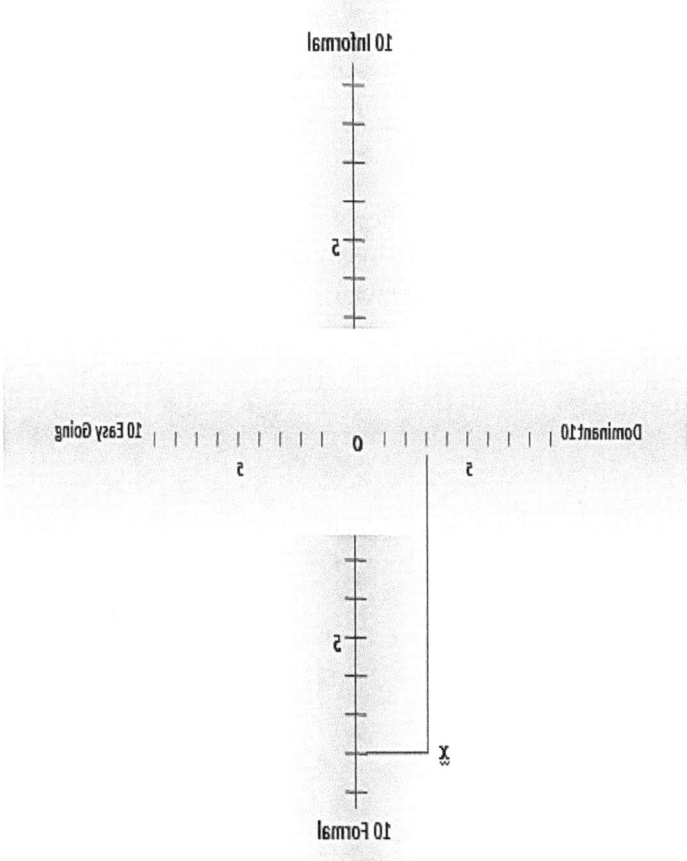

For example, a person whom you evaluate as an 8 on the formal continuum and a 3 on the Dominant continuum will have an "X" placed like the one above.

This evaluation will only take you a moment once you're familiar with the characteristics. You will "get" the information you need about a person after only a few moments of interaction.

Now the placement of the "X" takes on even more meaning. On each of the four directions are the characteristics you just considered and the "X" of the person you are evaluating. In each of the four quadrants of the target, we superimpose the four personality styles mentioned above expressive, amiable, driver, and analytical.

To determine a communication style (Expressive, Amiable, Driver or Analytical), we begin with the North vs. South and West vs. East chart and create a "target" image from it. That chart looks like this:

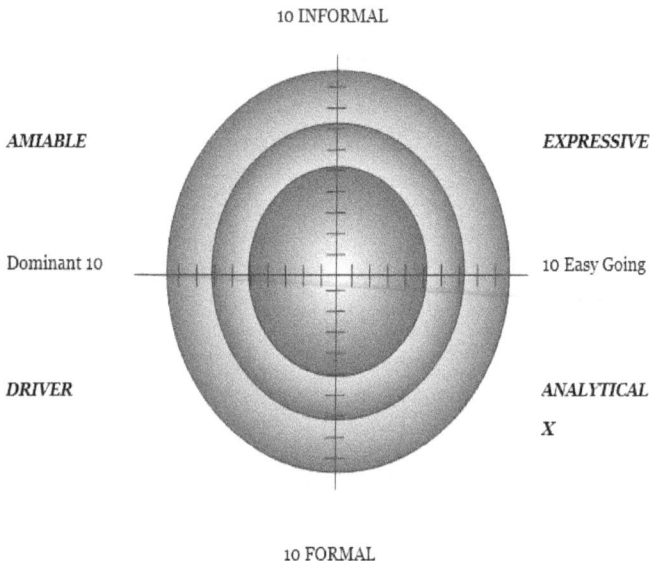

A person's communication style corresponds to their "X" that you located based on their personality characteristics. The person we identified uses a Driver communication style.

To repeat, personality characteristics (the way a person wants to be treated) determine their best communication style. The location of the person's "X" in one of the quadrants tells you their communication style and their placement toward the center or outer edge of the target tells you the depth, or extent of their personality in those characteristics.

Now you know the person's style and how completely they fit into that style, based on the position of their "X." Let's consider the communication style for each quadrant – each communication style.

Expressive

These people are highly dominant. They want to set the agenda and take the initiative. They give off lots of feeling and warmth – always trying to promote a new idea, a new thing, or themselves.

They:
- Are direct and expansive
- Are relationship-oriented and verbal
- Value activity and companionship
- Ask who questions
- Are desirous of flexibility
- Are dependent on their fun-loving nature
- Are fast paced and impulsive
- Want personal interaction
- Need incentives and endorsements
- Are proud of personal recognition
- Measure progress by applause and positive feedback

Now that you can identify a style and determine personality traits associated with their style, what do you do with the information? As an excellent communicator, you'll want to think about how each style WANTS TO BE TREATED. Whether you're sharing an idea, describing an opportunity, or simply making a lunch date, consider the "hot buttons" of each style and try to incorporate them into your communication.

Here's how that works for an Expressive.
- Support their dreams and goals
- Be stimulating and entertaining
- Provide testimony and incentives
- Allow time for socializing and relating
- Show your interest in their ideas
- Ask their opinions
- Move quickly and positively
- Keep the pace moving
- Build rapport and excitement
- Get agreement in writing
- Show enthusiasm for your ideas
- Show how your product enhances their self- esteem
- Remember their decisions are based on emotion
- They want to do things the easy way

To make your communication powerful, you can even pick the words the receiver likes best. You've undoubtedly heard that certain words have extraordinary power to influence reactions and emotions. When you consider personality styles, it makes sense that powerful words can be even more targeted and effective. Here is a list of words that will work for Expressive people. It will be particularly helpful when you're writing to people. Get them excited about the potential of your product and what it will do for them with these words. Remember to stimulate and entertain.

- Luxurious
- Exciting
- Dynamic
- Unique
- Different
- Entertaining

- Impressive
- Rewarding

Amiable

These people are easy going, relaxed in interpersonal settings, and highly informal. They exhibit lots of feeling and personality and have an accepting style, both giving acceptance and needing it in return.

They:
- Are indirect
- Are friendly and relationship-oriented
- Listen well
- Need assurances and guarantees
- Contribute support
- Depend on acceptance and loyalty
- Value respectful, supportive communication
- Cooperate in a slow, easy pace
- Desire trust and companionship
- Ask why questions
- Desire close relationships
- Appreciate the limelight and attention
- Measure progress by strokes and attention

Here's how an Amiable person WANTS TO BE TREATED:

- Support their feelings and relationships
- Be agreeable and understanding
- Provide assurances and guarantees
- Allow time for socializing
- Show your personal interest and support
- Ask "how" questions
- Move casually and informally
- Keep the pace slow

- Build trust and credibility
- Get agreement without pushing
- Show the human element in your ideas
- Reassure them often
- Remember, decisions are based on relationships
- Friendships are very important

Help them to see your product as a way to provide safety, comfort, and/or security for them with these words. Always be supportive and sincere.

- Comfortable
- Expect
- Traditional
- Warm
- Personal
- Secure
- Enjoyable
- Satisfying

Driver

These people are highly dominant   and formal.

They like to set the agenda and take charge and control of others. They are self- controlled. They like to organize and discipline situations, objects and people. Control and organization is their priority.

They:
- Are direct and forceful
- Lead others using task-orientation
- Value time
- Ask what and when questions
- Desire control and results
- Depend on leadership skills

- Are fast-paced, even urgent in action
- Need options and alternatives
- Contribute authority and leadership
- Take pride in their record and results
- Measure progress by results

Here's how a Driver WANTS TO BE TREATED:

- Support their conclusions and actions
- Be efficient, clear, specific and brief
- Provide options
- Stick to business and stay organized
- Demonstrate your competence
- Ask specific questions – "What?"
- Move confidently and quickly
- Keep the pace purposeful and upbeat
- Build respect and credibility
- Get agreements by providing options
- Show net results of your ideas
- Build respect and credibility
- Show how your product will help reach their goals
- Remember, decisions are based on personal evaluation
- They want to save time

Be clear and concise with your words, proving that your product will meet their needs and make them successful using these words. Be effective and results oriented.

- Proven
- Tested
- Functional
- Dynamic
- Versatile
- Efficient
- Powerful

- Enviable

Analytical

These people are highly formal and self- disciplined. They are methodical and logical and usually easier going in a casual setting as opposed to a business one. They delight in analysis of and involvement with data.

They:
- Are indirect and reserved
- Are task-oriented and studious
- Value reliable plans
- Desire preparation
- Need details, facts and documentation
- Are deliberate and steady-paced
- Want to understand and process details
- Depend on accuracy
- Take pride in precise, active production
- Measure results by activity

Here's how an Analytical person WANTS TO BE TREATED:
- Support their principles and thinking
- Be accurate and patient
- Provide written data and evidence
- Stick to business
- Give pros and cons
- Move methodically and logically
- Keep the pace steady and organized
- Build with documentation
- Get agreements patiently and logically
- Show the logic and validity in your ideas
- Show how your product makes sense
- Remember, decisions are based on evaluation of facts

- They hate to be wrong or look bad

Choose your words carefully with an Analytical person because they will be paying attention. Be organized and prepared. Document your ideas with these words like the following.

- Practical
- Logical
- Validated
- Concise
- Realistic
- Economical
- High quality

What is your style? Consider yourself in terms of the descriptors above and mark the chart in your workbook based on your assessment. Remember to mark on the continuum from 0 to 10 with 0 being not very much that way and 10 being very much that way. Are you more Dominant or Easy Going? More Formal or Informal? Based on your "X" what is your communication style? If you're not objective enough to answer these important questions about yourself, ask people who know you, both in personal and professional relationships, to help place you.

Now, think of at least four friends/relatives/associates, and rate them first on the crosshairs chart, and then determine their communication style on the target. Will you change the way you communicate with them now that you're clear about the way they want to be treated? Does this shed some light on why your previous communications have worked well... or not?

Once you've done this process several times, it should begin to feel fairly easy. You'll find that a quick "targeting" exercise that you do in your head will often help tremendously when you're meeting someone who you'd like to communicate well with as soon as possible.

Considering your preferred communication style compared to the people you've evaluated, how far must you come across the chart from your own style and to meet other people's in order to treat them as they'd like to be treated. Your best communication will result from your own style not "getting in your way" as you strive to reach another person.

Clearly, the easiest communication will come between two people whose styles are very similar. They won't have to work very hard to get through to each other. However, if you are a Driver or an Expressive (as most entrepreneurs are) working with an Amiable or Analytical (as many employees are), you'll need to be particularly aware of what you say and how you say it.

It has been said that the very best communicators are those who have "chameleon-like" styles. These people's "Xs" are very close to the center of the target, so they move easily among the different styles and characteristics. They are adept, not insincere, because they have a little bit of everybody in themselves – as do we all!

In the last section, we will consider the more advanced communication skills you need to be successful as a leader and to maintain the best possible relationships in your life.

Using Powerful Communication Skills to Succeed

Let's look at how to achieve more success as a leader and get more out of your relationships, your work, and your life through powerful communication skills.

> *"The art of communication is the language of leadership."* — *James Humes*

Your success at communicating determines your success in business as well as in life. It's as simple – and important– as that. This book was created to heighten your awareness and give you a deeper look at the process of communication that will enable you to have stronger, more effective relationships. In this final lesson, we will examine the impact of communication on your role as a leader. We'll also consider various communication strategies that you need to employ in order to meet your entrepreneurial goals. Since this book is all about taking you to the next level as a powerful communicator – let's crank those concepts up a notch!

> *"Developing excellent communication skills is absolutely essential to effective leadership. The leader must be able to share knowledge and ideas to transmit a sense of urgency and enthusiasm to others. If a leader can't get a message across clearly and motivate others to act on it, then having a message doesn't even matter."*
> — *Gilbert Amelio, President and CEO of National Semiconductor Corp.*

Selling Yourself

Whether you're in sales professionally or not, as a leader and entrepreneur, you're constantly selling yourself. You must get other people to "buy" your ideas, your plans, your goals, and your solutions. You can learn to understand your "audience," be it one person or many, by using the rapport and relationship concepts you've learned in this book. Then, your job will be much easier and your success more assured.

One of the ways you'll be able to sell yourself consistently is by establishing trust with your listeners. You've learned about the impact that good rapport has on all levels of communication. Without it, there can be no trust. The key to building rapport and trust is accurate and effective communication. Trust is one of the basic requirements to getting another person to "buy" your idea, product, service, or suggestion. Therefore, your efforts to increase trust are always worthwhile.

> *"Speech is power: speech is to persuade, to convert, to compel. It is to bring another out of his bad sense into your good sense."*
> *– Ralph Waldo Emerson*

Vocabulary and Grammar

> *"One of the most important qualities of successful leaders is an ability to express thoughts and knowledge. Research by management and human resource experts confirms that no matter what the field of employment, people with large vocabularies - those able to speak clearly and concisely, using simple as well as descriptive words - are best at accomplishing their goals. Well chosen, carefully considered words can close the sale, negotiate the raise, enhance relationships, and change destinies." – Denis Waitley*

A great vocabulary is a priceless possession. It would be well worth your time to spend the rest of your life building your collection of words. When you come across one that you don't know, take the time to look it up and make it your own by using it several times. You may be surprised at the things you learn in the meaning of one word.

Grammar and spelling may be a challenge for you that you don't even know you have. Depending on your education, and the emphasis that was placed on grammar and spelling as you went through school and at home, you may be making more errors than you realize, particularly when you write. The importance of grammar and spelling in your writing can't be overstated. If you have any concern about how you're presenting yourself in this area, consider taking an English or writing course to measure what you know and expand your skills.

Email

If you're the sender, emails are very serious; if you're the receiver, don't take them seriously at all. As a powerful communicator, it's important for you to understand the potential – and the limitations – of email.

The limitations can be profound. As you know, only 7% of an interaction's meaning is derived from the words exchanged. Email therefore leaves 93% of the communication hanging in cyberspace! That's quite a bit to be left to the imagination! Have you ever received an email that sounded like the writer was yelling at you or mad at you or didn't care?

This is a common result of the staccato style of email. It's also often a reflection on the sender's poor writing skills. The feelings and mood and even intentions of the senders are typically not a part of the communication, which leaves the receiver feeling conflicted about the intent of the message.

Here's an important rule of thumb for you: If you have a sensitive or important message to deliver, go see the person –

or, at least, pick up the phone, to deliver it. That way, you can answer questions and sense their feelings and needs.

Here's another dynamic of email. When you send an email, you are putting a message in writing. It is therefore transferable – and could be sent around the planet! Before hitting send, there are some things you should consider. First, is this a message that you want in writing? And, in an office or professional setting, it is a potentially poor way to communicate? If messages can be misconstrued or if they can find their way into the wrong hands, maybe they shouldn't be emailed. Second, how are you representing yourself and your reputation? Be careful about the words you choose, the spelling and punctuation, and even style, which represent to other people who you are.

On the positive side, email and instant messaging are obviously convenient methods of communication – and often better than none. In some cases, they can even enhance communication and a relationship when used to stay in touch. In our global business world, the email you send at noon is probably preferable to a phone call to your colleague on the other side of the planet at midnight his time. Just keep in mind that they are not a substitution for person-to-person contact or a way to deliver sensitive messages. The old adage, "think before you speak," certainly applies to email.

Take a look at your email in and out boxes. Can you find examples of messages that you could have written better–
or shouldn't have written at all? What about messages you received? What impressions did you get about the senders?

Cell Phones

Cell phones are one of the entrepreneur's most important tools. They obviously allow you to stay on top of the many projects and situations you're managing. They allow you to stay informed and keep others informed. They allow you to reach out to associates and employees and keep them motivated and productive.

The only reminder that busy entrepreneurs sometimes need is common courtesy. Rapport that you have built with a person can be damaged when you receive or place cell calls in their presence that are disruptive, steal time and appear rude. Don't allow your cell phone to get in the way of personal interactions, manners, and even your public image. Cell phones and busy highways also create – room for error.

Feedback

"Leaders who make it a practice to draw out the thoughts and ideas of their subordinates and who are receptive even to bad news will be properly informed. Communicate downward to subordinates with at least the same care and attention as you communicate upward to superiors." - - L. B. Belker

One of the most important demands on your communication skills happens around feedback. As a skilled communicator, you need to use it both to give and receive information about how well the work is going, how satisfied people are with the work and how well they understand the tasks at hand, as well as how well you are communicating and relating to another person, or group.

Feedback is a powerful communication tool in that it can help you learn about how you come across to others. It can also enable you to course-correct when you learn more about how your messages are being received. Your willingness to hear feedback is very important. When you create an open atmosphere for others to offer feedback, you're laying the groundwork for this important process to unfold.

Receiving Feedback
Welcome constructive feedback. As long as the feedback comes to you in a non-judgmental and appropriate fashion, accept it is as a valuable piece of information for learning and for your continued development as a leader.

Here are some points to remember when you receive feedback:
- Accept it for what it is – information.
- Evaluate it before responding.
- Make your own choice about what you intend to do with the information.

You can use another person's complaints as a tool to create an open atmosphere. One way is by putting what the other person has said into your own words and reflecting it back. This technique is known as paraphrasing.

Paraphrasing another person's feedback is a good way to show that you are listening and understanding. For example, you could say:

"So what I hear you saying is…." or, "Your idea is…" or, "My understanding of what you're suggesting is…"

Giving Feedback
As a leader, you can help other people improve their communication skills, as well as help them to communicate better with you, by offering feedback as well as asking for it.

Giving feedback can be one of the most difficult situations in communication. Without knowing how to give feedback, it can be uncomfortable and unpleasant for both the giver and the receiver. But, it doesn't have to be if you keep these tips in mind.

- Stay positive. Constructive feedback can motivate people, while negative comments can be counter-productive, demotivating and destructive.

- Offer praise for those aspects of the job that are well done. Reinforce the behavior that is good and appropriate. In this case you can identify the good behavior with the person. Use their name, and tell them what's working.

- Offer it in a way that the receiver can use it to either make improvements or keep up the good work. Limit your comments to one or two important points – not trying to cover too much at one time.

- Share specific information that provides the recipient guidance and direction in an activity. Tell him or her what you suggest as a different behavior or approach.

- Giving feedback is an integral part of the coaching process that provides your staff members with support and direction, and ultimately results in increased participation. Both positive and negative feedbacks have their part to play. It is the best way to convey to your staff what you think about a particular work or performance.

- Choose correct timing for feedback. Feedback is most helpful and effective when given at the earliest opportunity after the given behavior or incident has occurred. Immediate feedback will help to reinforce a correct behavior and make it more likely to happen again. Constructive feedback also is most effective when given as soon as possible after it is needed.

- Focus on specifics. Feedback should *not* be linked to the personality or character of the person. Focus on a specific correct or incorrect behavior. Such feedback can make a person more willing and able to change. Feedback should be specific, visible and measurable in order to be effective. Cite a particular case or example so you're very clear about what you liked or what could be done differently.

- Listen to their feelings and ideas regarding your feedback. Make sure they understand by asking them to summarize or paraphrase your interaction.

Who are some people you would like to give feedback to as soon as possible? Begin that valuable process by planning for it now.

The Most Powerful Communication of All...

"The most basic and powerful way to connect to another person is to listen. Just listen. Perhaps the most important thing we ever give each other is our attention.... A loving silence often has far more power to heal and to connect than the most well-intentioned words." – Rachel N. Reman

You can say more with actions than you ever will with words. The most powerful communication happens when you SHOW another person or other people that you are who you say you are; that you love them; that you care about them; that you will do as you have promised. Consider the messages that come with one of the most precious gifts we can offer – our time.

There are times that no words can say what a hug or a handshake can say. Remember the power you have to communicate with your actions.

> *"The way we communicate with others and with ourselves ultimately determines the quality of our lives."*
> - *Tony Robbins*

What specific ideas have you learned that will help you communicate better with people you lead in business and professional interactions?

What ways can you think of to SHOW people you work with, business associates and loved ones who you are and what matters in your relationship?

Consider the people you communicate with regularly. Write their names in the first column of the chart below. Beside each name, evaluate how well you think your communication usually flows with that person. In the third column, make a few notes about what you think you can do to improve communication with that person. When will you make the changes?

Name	Quality: Excellent, Good, Marginal or Poor	Changes I can make...

Revisiting the Communication Evaluator

Now that you have spent time and effort improving your communication skills, please evaluate yourself again using this quiz. Then, add one point for each check. If you haven't had enough time to put your new skills to work, you might want to re-evaluate your progress again in 30 days.

The Communication Evaluator Part II

Communication Basics

- ☐ I believe that the more powerful my communications, the better.
- ☐ I'm a confident communicator.
- ☐ I know how to listen actively.
- ☐ I rarely interrupt other people.
- ☐ I rarely have communication mix-ups or challenges.

Basics score out of 5: _____

Communication Challenges

- ☐ Other people clearly understand my communication most of the time.
- ☐ The outcomes and results that happen after I make a request or give an instruction are most often those I expect.
- ☐ I'm comfortable meeting new people.
- ☐ I can keep a conversation going with someone I just met.
- ☐ I can always be proud of my written communication.
- ☐ I communicate with people easily, regardless of their personality style.
- ☐ People seem to feel better about me and about themselves after our communications.
- ☐ I know how to ask questions when I need clarification.
- ☐ I'm familiar with the filters that get in the way of people hearing my messages.
- ☐ I'm aware of communication challenges that keep coming up for me and what to do about them.

Challenges score out of 10: ____

Communicating to Groups

- ☐ I often speak to groups of people.
- ☐ I look forward to speaking to groups because that format of communication is often important.
- ☐ When I speak to people, I feel confident and positive.
- ☐ When I speak to people, I get a chance to get my ideas across.
- ☐ When I speak to people, I receive good feedback.

Groups score out of 5: _____

Communicating Professionally

- ☐ I'm comfortable giving feedback to people who work with and for me.
- ☐ I'm comfortable receiving feedback from peers and employees.
- ☐ My instructions to others are consistently followed and completed, as I need them to be.
- ☐ My peers share their ideas and goals and seem eager to hear mine.
- ☐ I can quickly "figure out" how to approach other people about business.

Professional score out of 5: _____

Communicating as a Leader

- ☐ I believe that clear communication is a crucially important aspect of leadership.
- ☐ I'm confident working with other people at meetings.
- ☐ I lead efficient, clear and productive meetings.
- ☐ I'm confident that when I communicate new ideas and goals to people I lead, they will become excited and contribute to the goals.

☐ When I speak as a leader, people respect what I have to say.

Leadership score out of 5: _____

Scoring

Overall Score	
Basics	
Challenges	
Groups	
Professional	
Leadership	
TOTAL:	

Notice the areas that your communication skills need the most work. The chart below will interpret your current feelings about yourself as a communicator.

Evaluation	
27-30	You believe you have a solid mastery of communication, while there may be room for improvement.
20-26	Good communication skills are indicated with a few areas that need work.
15-19	Your communication ability needs work – Keep working with this book to strengthen your areas of weakness.
0-14	Powerful communication is a challenge for you, but keep using the tools and information here and you'll see improvement in no time!

Conclusion

Congratulations on your efforts to improve your skills and to become a Powerful Communicator. I hope you've found the book and the topic interesting and valuable.

The ultimate value will come from your application of these ideas and theories. Good luck. All of your efforts will be worthwhile and – I know you'll start seeing the results immediately!

Ric Thompson

Check out these other titles by Ric Thompson...

http://www.amazon.com/dp/B00H4HHY56

http://www.amazon.com/dp/B00I3Q2QPK

http://www.amazon.com/dp/B00LIGKRCG